Bert, His Dog, Our God

Love thy Neighbour

'You shall love your neighbour as yourself'

(Matthew 22: 39)

GARY BUNT

with

Leslie J. Francis and Phillip Vernon

Bear Lands Publishing

About Bert and his dog

Bert and his dog invite us to go on a journey of discovery, on a journey of encounter, as they meet with Jesus in unexpected landscapes. These landscapes link us with the Gospel narratives, and draw us into deeper encounters with the transformative power of the Christian tradition.

Bert and his dog invite us to join them in these evocative encounters.

About this series of books

This series of books has been designed in celebration of the centenary of the consecration of Liverpool Cathedral in 1924 by Gary Bunt (Liverpool Cathedral Centenary Artist) and Leslie J. Francis (Liverpool Cathedral Canon Theologian).

Gary Bunt is represented by Portland Gallery, London.

Canon Leslie J. Francis is Professor of Religions, Psychology and Education, Bishop Grosseteste University, Lincoln.

Published 2022 by Bear Lands Publishing, The St Mary's Centre, Llys Onnen, Abergwyngregyn, Gwynedd, LL33 0LD, Wales.

Copyright © Gary Bunt (art and poem), Leslie J. Francis (interpretation), Phillip Vernon (design).

First published 2022.

ISBN 978-1-9115143-8-1

Printed by www.gekkocreative.co.uk

Setting the scene

In Matthew's Gospel, chapter 22, the people who hold the power were out to trap Jesus. The Pharisee tried to trap Jesus with a political question, about paying taxes. The Sadducee tried to trap Jesus with a theological question, about life after death. The lawyer tried to trap Jesus with a legal question, about priorities within the law of Moses. In response to the question asked by the lawyer, Jesus offers his well known 'summary of the law'.

The greatest and the first commandment

Hear, O Israel: The Lord is our God, the Lord alone.

You shall love the Lord your God with all your heart,

and with all your soul, and with all your might.

Keep these words that I am commanding you

today in your heart.

Recite them to your children and talk

about them when you are at home

and when you are away,

when you lie down

and when you rise.

Deuteronomy 6: 4-7 (NRSV)

And a second commandment is like it

A lawyer, asked Jesus a question to test him.
'Teacher, which commandment in the law is the greatest?'
He said to him,
"You shall love the Lord your God with all your heart,
and with all your soul, and with all your mind."
This is the greatest and first commandment.
And a second is like it:
"You shall love your neighbour as yourself."
On these two commandments
hang all the law and the prophets.'
Matthew 22: 35-40 (NRSV)

Look carefully at the picture

Draw on your senses (sensing)

- What details in the picture catch your attention?
- What can you see?
- What can you hear?
- What can you touch?
- What can you smell?
- What can you taste?
- What does Jesus' posture say?

Look carefully at the picture

Draw on your imagination (intuition)

- What ideas does the picture spark in your mind?
- What connections can you make with your personal experience?
- What big themes intrigue you?
- What is going on in the dog's mind?
- What is going on in the cat's mind?

Look carefully at the picture

Draw on your heart (feeling)

- What most touches your heart in the picture?
- Put yourself in the cat's situation, how is the cat feeling?
- Put yourself in the dog's situation, how is the dog feeling?
- When have you shared the cat's feeling?
- When have you shared the dog's feeling?

Look carefully at the picture

Draw on your mind (thinking)

- What most stretches your mind in the picture?
- What questions and issues are raised in your mind?
- What does the first commandment mean to you?
- What does the second commandment mean to you?
- How relevant are these two commandments for life today?

Love thy neighbour

Today I was given a lesson

I had to raise my paw

And swear that I would try my best

To uphold an important law

Love thy neighbour as thyself

I was okay with that

But there's a rule of mine where I draw the line

In loving next door's cat

Putting yourself in the picture

- Have you felt under threat from someone really different from you?
- Have you felt strong dislike for someone really different from you?
- How can you best learn to live with difference and diversity?

Shaping your responses

Reflecting on this picture

- What might you remember most?
- What might you decide to do?
- What will you find most difficult to do?
- What might you say in your prayers?

Bert and his dog

Bert and his dog continue on their journey
of discovery, on their journey of encounter.
Where might they next meet with Jesus
in an unexpected landscape?